Do Something Different In Your Salon Today!

Steve Hilliard

What Industry Insiders Are Saying About 'Do Something Different In Your Salon Today'

Simple and Concise.

'Having worked with Steve for many years, it's always been clear he's consistently looking for ways to improve his business and avoid the mistakes many salon owners make when they only take action if something goes wrong (... which is generally too late!)

His ability to explain his ideas in a simple and concise manner makes it easy for busy salon owners to focus on what's important to their business and implement his proven effective strategies – highly recommended!'

Mark Rowley from Shortcuts Salon Software

Hacks that really make a difference.

Having the pleasure of working with Steve Hilliard over the years its fantastic that Steve has found time to put down in words what has made him, his team and his business so successful so other salon owners who also want to strive for excellence can follow in his footsteps.

Steve has that rare ability to clearly communicate in the simplest forms true business "hacks" which really make a difference. Try them ... and see for yourself!

Mark Giannandrea General Manager UK Goldwell

I wish I'd read it years ago!

OMG I feel this book was written just for me, it's so easy to read and helpful … I wish I'd read it years ago.

Why?

Because before I read it, I was full time on the floor thinking I had to be busy for the salon to survive, I was feeling old, stressed out and knackered and because I didn't have time to manage my staff properly they were doing pretty much what they wanted. This worked for them but not my business!

Steve's book has given me the answers I needed and a clear plan to follow … every salon owner should read it!

Liz from Vogue International.

Thankyou Steve for a five-star read.

I found "Do Something Different In Your Salon Today" by Steve Hillard, to be very well put together and really simple to follow. I read it in under two hours, but I feel I've have gained two years knowledge in that short time.

Understanding and implementing Salon targets was something I've been struggling with for some time and Steve has helped me loads with that.

In summary it's a positive read for anyone starting a salon and more experienced owners as well. Everyone can benefit understanding how to organise their salon so it's easy to run.

Thank you Steve for a five-star read.

Catherine McElligott from The Hairshop

I can't wait for the next one!!

I've just finished Do Something Different! It was such an inspirational read and being a salon owner myself I can relate to everything Steve says. I will certainly take on some of the techniques he's shared in this book and I'd highly recommend all salon owners to read it!

I can't wait for the next one!!

Steph from First Impressions

Acknowledgements

I'd like to begin by paying tribute to my Mum and Dad for the start they gave me in life and in particular I dedicate this book to the memory of my Dad for the gift of inspiration he gave me to 'Do' and 'Be' more, which you'll find at the heart of everything I now share with you in these pages.

I'd also like to publicly thank my wife and family for their love and support over the years… it can't have been easy at times!

I'd like to show my appreciation to my current and former team members because you've all played a part and I couldn't have done it without you.

Finally, I'd like to thank Simon Lotinga for his invaluable help in getting my ideas down on paper and this first book published!

Contents

Introduction

I'm sure you'll be pleased to know, this book has been written for Salon Owners by a Salon Owner.

If you're a Salon Owner too, you're going to love it... especially if you're feeling trapped, stressed out or simply fed up that the same staff, client or money problems seem to keep happening again and again… and you don't know why.

The good news is, what you're feeling at the moment isn't rare, in fact **most** **Salon Owners start feeling the same way, somewhere between 3 and 7 years after they open for business** and I'll explain why in a minute.

Before I do, I want you to know I've kept his book brief and to the point and I promise it isn't full of business jargon either, so you'll discover you can read it easily in a couple of hours.

Don't let the fact that it's an easy read fool you, because the book contains advice gained from a lot of hard earned experience and it can make a real difference - **if you do something different with it!**

I've written it for you, because I know how you feel. I know because I've felt the same way myself, which means I'm painfully aware of what it's like... *I also know that once I started 'doing' the business of running my salon and working with my staff in a different way, everything changed and I've never looked back.*

When I was feeling as you are now, I was very frustrated and it took me ages to realise what was really happening, then understand and believe I could **'do'** running my salon in a different way.

Now I want to help you understand and believe as well.

Before I begin, let me prove I understand where you are now by sharing a little of my salon owning story with you.

Although my career began in 1986, it was 1996 before I took the plunge and opened my first salon.

The decision to do it started with a feeling... **a feeling that I was being held back and that I could do better.**

Did you ever feel that?

When I thought about it, I realised it was because I was having to conform to someone else's vision and as much as I loved my job and respected my employer, the little voice in the back of my head kept telling me that **my** vision of a salon would deliver a better service and build a stronger brand.

So, there I was in 1996 with a head full of beliefs and the only way to prove if I was right or not to myself, was to take a brave pill and set out on my own... **so I did!**

The good news is, my little voice **was** right because my new salon got busy very quickly.

The bad news was that I soon became by far the busiest stylist, which meant I was so wrapped up in the process of delivering an amazing service to my clients that I had to fit managing my staff and dealing with all my business responsibilities in the gaps between appointments, or as often happened… **when the salon was closed!**

In the early days, it didn't matter too much… the excitement of having my own business made it all worthwhile, but bit by bit I grew tired, fed up, disillusioned with the treadmill I was on, working, working, working, always feeling knackered!

Many times, I said to myself there's got to be a better way than this, but every time I tried to get organised, pull away and delegate to others a problem or crisis would crop up and I'd be sucked back in.

I became frustrated with my business, frustrated paying my stylists good money to sit around and watch me work, frustrated to be busy and yet not truly **UNDERSTAND** how to make it all work FOR me.

I had to do something, the question was… what?

I began speaking to lots of other salon owners at conferences and events and was shocked to discover I wasn't alone… **MOST SALON OWNERS FELT MUCH THE SAME WAY!**

Determined to find the answer I bought books (*and I'll share details of the ones that helped me most as we go along*), I also went on courses & listened to CDs but for a while nothing really changed.

Looking back, I now understand it's because I was looking for answers outside myself. I thought I needed to change my business to make it work.

WRONG!!!

What I really needed to change was **me.**

By that I mean my attitudes, beliefs, habits and ultimately my behaviour… or to put it another way… **what I was DOING in the salon every day.**

The first clue to this understanding came in a book I began reading on holiday called **The Botty Rules.**

The author Nigel Botterill had built several, *million pound plus turnover* businesses and in his book he was sharing his golden rules for success.

His first golden rule was… **"Take 90 minutes a day away from your customers to work on your business."**

Now in itself this wasn't new knowledge… in fact I'd go so far as to say it was just plain common sense. What was new to me however was the **attitude** he insisted you **had** to bring to those 90 minutes a day.

The ninety minutes were **NOT** to be used for popping down to the cash and carry.

NOT to be used to catch up with your paperwork.

NOT to be used for talking to reps or staff members who wanted a pay rise or just to have a moan.

Instead it was to be used to work on understanding your numbers.

Understanding how to motivate and lead your team.

Understanding how to create and deliver a compelling marketing message that creates a flood of raving fan clients of the salon… not just it's superstar stylists.

In other words, the **90 minutes** a day was for strategic, financial, operational and marketing planning and implementation … **not short-term firefighting and problem solving.**

It was **90 minutes** for being a bold business owner **not** a busy manager or stylist.

90 minutes for developing into the leader I needed to become to create a business that worked **FOR** me, instead of just giving me a stressful job.

Now I'll be totally honest here… I could see the sense in what he was saying but part of me was scared.

- *Scared of what my clients would say.*

- *Scared of losing the valuable turnover I brought to the business.*

- *Scared I might not be good enough, because it really would need me to step up and be a different sort of salon owner.*

I might have been a bit scared, but I was also excited because I could finally see this was my chance to '**DO**' something in a totally different way and I grabbed it with both hands.

I'm pleased to say… I've never looked back!

Now let's be clear here. Nigel had never been a salon owner. There was **nothing** in his book that was salon specific. In fact, to make his ideas work I had to take his general principles and adapt them to create salon specific answers.

As I did, I found his general principles were very practical and my first salon specific change was **to RULE out the 90 minutes a day he suggested to work on my business.**

My clients accepted my restricted appointment hours easily and the confidence I took from the success of spending 90 minutes a day working on my business rather than my clients, fuelled of a process of amazing change in my salon.

Remember it was only possible because I had the courage to **'do something different'** even if it was scary.

I'm talking about changes like my staff problems melting away as the group of people who'd caused me, so many problems began working well together as they developed into a stable happy team who produced good **profits** and caused me **very** few problems.

Now if you're still in the getting it wrong phase, don't worry, we've agreed it's not surprising and it does happen to nearly everyone.

The good news is you just have to **believe** there's an alternative, believe you can **'do something different'** and everything will start to change for you as well.

That's what this book is for.

**To show you how to do something different in your salon...
starting today!**

Why is it so important?

**Because, if you keep on doing what you've always done,
you'll keep on getting what you've always got!**

For your salon owning results and experience to change,
what you **'DO'** has to change.

When you **'DO'** start doing the different things I share with
you in this book, the feeling of pride, profit and satisfaction
you get, will be life changing!

Now before we get stuck into the meat of the book, I want to
share an important issue with you.

It's something that <u>didn't</u> apply to me, but **DOES** apply to
most salon owners so there's a good chance you're affected
by it.

I believe the fact it doesn't apply to me is why I was able to
work things out for myself and transform my salon.

It's also why I was able to become a successful coach who
loves nothing more than helping salon owners **'do something
different'** in their salons... while their competitors struggle to
make any progress!

The good news is, if it does apply to you and you are being

affected by it, **'doing something different'** will give you the answers you need to finally get unstuck and start making real progress.

By now you're probably curious so let me explain.

The issue I'm talking about is the fact that most salon owners start their business for the <u>wrong</u> reason.

When I say the wrong reason, I don't mean we don't have a good reason, because most of them are **very** good reasons and most of them motivate us very powerfully... **in the beginning.**

But it's the **in the beginning** bit where the problem lies.

Let me explain.

Motivation is a word which is used to describe something that gets you to take action.

It can be broken down into 2 very simple categories:

1. **'Towards'** *motivation.*

2. **'Away'** *motivation.*

This is because as human beings we're either attracted to move **towards** something we want; like the warm fuzzy feelings we get when we see something attractive or buy something nice. Or we find ourselves repelled and move <u>away</u> from something we don't want; like negative feelings, pain, or the fear of losing something we love or value!

Does that make sense?

So which type of motivation got **you** to make the decision to become the owner of a hairdressing business?

Let's look at the most common reasons I'm given when I ask the salon owners I'm coaching this question, and see if any match your own experience:

- *You may have worked for a salon owner who wanted to sell up, or retire and they needed someone to take the business over, so it could carry on. Now, because you're already there working as an employee and because you* **'know'** *the business, you decide its* **'safe'** *to buy it.*

- *Or you may have been in the same situation as above, with an owner who wants to move on. Taking on a salon was* **not** *something you ever considered or really wanted, but now you feel under pressure to do it. Why? Because if you don't, everyone including* **you** *will need to find new jobs ... so you buy the business.*

- *Or you may have been a successful stylist who got to the point where you felt worth more than any boss was prepared (or could afford) to pay you,* **so you leave and open your own salon, so you can take control of what you earn.**

- *Or you may have been a successful stylist who got fed up with feeling de-motivated, and being taken for granted. Fed up with working in a bitchy atmosphere and being managed badly. Finally, it gets so bad you decide to start your own salon ...* **where you promise yourself things will be different.**

- *Or you may have had a client, a parent or a friend with money who kept telling you, **'you can do it'** and was prepared to put some or all the money up. Because of their **'belief'** in you and the fact that the money's available, **you decide to start your own salon.***

There are plenty of other reasons we could talk about. These are the most common, and they're all **very** good, **very** normal, **very** understandable reasons, that get us to take action and either buy an existing business or start one from scratch.

So, what's the problem?

Try thinking about it this way; all the reasons we've just talked about are 'away' motivation reasons. Why? In each case it's because the trigger for starting or buying a salon was **'outside'** of you. This means it's highly likely you started your salon because **someone else** decided to either...

- *move on*

- *guilt trip you into doing it*

- *not value you enough*

- *value **you** more than you do **yourself***

- *or simply behave badly towards you.*

Put that way it's a bit of an eye opener, isn't it!

So, what's the problem with buying or starting a salon using **'away'** motivation? Well, it's all a question of energy and focus.

'**Away**' motivation is good for making things happen. It's good for beginnings, but the problem with away motivation is simple... **its effects don't <u>last</u>!**

'**Away**' motivation gives us the reason to get started; but after the initial excitement and adrenaline rush of getting everything organised and opening our doors to paying clients, the '**what's next**' question needs answering. And we do answer it: **Sort of!**

Why only sort of?

Because in the early days of growing your business, you're still trying to get on top everything, aren't you; so '**what's next**' normally boils down to getting more established, which means getting...

- ***more*** *clients*
- *more staff*
- ***more*** *turnover*
- ***more*** *profit.*

This is fine for a while, but without a clear long-term vision or goal to focus on, your attention will naturally **<u>stay</u>** on the never-ending stream of client, staff and money challenges that every small business owner has to face.

When your focus stays on short term problems like these, you're in real danger of falling into what I call the '**hamster on a wheel syndrome**' and if that happens you'll feel like you're **working very hard but going nowhere.**

Now think about this... if **'away'** motivation eventually leads to hamster on a wheel syndrome, does **'towards'** motivation really have the answer?

Yes... and I'm living proof!

If you remember I had a strong **'towards motivation'** vision for my business right from the beginning and this is **WHY** I believe I had the drive strength and determination to **'start doing things differently'** and break out of the hamster wheel syndrome that holds so many salon owners back.

The good news is, it's never too late to create a tidal wave of **'towards motivation'** for you, your team and your clients and as you discover the secrets to **'doing something different in your salon'** in this book you'll understand why.

CHAPTER 1

'DO' work on <u>YOU</u> first!

Have you ever watched people like Gordon Ramsey, John Harvey Jones, Alex Polizzi, or Tabatha Coffey trying to sort out troubled businesses on TV?

If you haven't**... I respectfully suggest you <u>should!</u>**

When you do, you'll see them struggling to help businesses with all sorts of problems but look closely and you'll see that underneath **<u>ALL</u>** the problems there is usually **one** underlying cause.

The attitudes, beliefs and behaviour of the owner of the business.

You could say, *and I often do*, **"Your business is a reflection of you".** In fact, it's a reflection of your **'self-image'** (*how you see yourself*) and your self-image is dramatically affected by the state of your self-esteem (*how you feel about yourself.*)

This means businesses that have recurring problems nearly always have owners with self-esteem and self-image challenges running them.

If this applies to you then **'DO'** work on this and I have to be honest and tell you that you won't do it without a fight, and **fighting can be uncomfortable**, can't it... so be prepared!

The first thing you have to fight for is your belief in yourself.

Why?

- *Because belief comes before confidence: **Your confidence.***

- *Confidence comes before action: **Your action.***

- *Action comes before success: **Your success and acting, by definition, requires you to 'DO' something!***

If you want proof that your self-esteem could be behind your problems, just answer the following question... In your Salon, do any of the following statements apply to you?

- *Nothing gets done unless you nag.*

- *You find it easier to do things yourself.*

- *You find it hard to put up prices because you don't want to lose clients or deal with the moans from your staff.*

- *Your staff room atmosphere is quite bitchy.*

- *You find it hard to confront '**difficult**' people.*

- *You keep losing staff.*

- *Your salon struggles to grow.*

- *You find it hard to trust some of your staff.*

- *You can be moody or stressed out at work.*

The truth is, if you answered yes to even **one** of these statements, low self-esteem and a poor self-image are affecting you and I strongly believe you **have** to do something about it!

You have to 'DO' the work needed to improve them as a matter of urgency.

When you **'DO'** the work consistently, **everything** else we're going to talk about becomes possible. Put off doing it, as many of you will, and you'll find the other ideas I'm going to share with you simply won't work.

In other words, a positive self-image and the high self-esteem that go with it are **the** foundation for everything else you want.

How can a poor self-image be so damaging?

Think of it like the **'Windows'** operating software on a computer. When it's working properly, your computer can do fantastic things. When it isn't, **nothing** works the way it should and you find yourself wasting time, getting frustrated and going around in circles.

Your self-image controls **your** operating software, which is made up of...

- *your emotions*

- *your beliefs*

- *your habits.*

Your emotions can be positive or negative, and we all live with a mixture of both, but in the same way a computer has a **'safe'** mode to revert to when things go wrong, your subconscious mind has a **'safe'** emotional response to fall back on when you're under pressure!

Let me show you how damaging it is for our **'safe'** emotions to be negative; and we'd better start by looking at what the most common negative emotions are...

- *anger*

- *fear*

- *guilt*

- *sadness*

- *hurt.*

Now let's make these negative emotions come alive.

We all know people who get **'angry':**

- *They blow up for the slightest reason, don't they?*

- *They're often bullies, aren't they? And we respond to them in different ways depending on the state of our own self-image.*

- *We either choose to confront them, avoid them completely, or walk on eggshells if we **'have'** to deal with them!*

We all know people who are ruled by **'fear':**

- *We know they can be indecisive, hard to motivate and absolutely __hate__ confrontation.*

- *They may be frightened of failure or getting things wrong, **so they don't take risks.***

- *They may be frightened of success, **so they sabotage anything that starts to go well because they think they don't 'deserve' it.***

- *They may be frightened of looking silly, being seen as cocky or standing out from the crowd.*

- *They may be afraid people won't like them, **so they try to 'please' everyone.***

We all know people who are driven by **'guilt'**:

- *No matter what they do, they feel **'guilty'** about not **'doing'** enough, or not being **'good'** enough.*

- *More often than not their guilt drives them to be impossible to help, or please, or even worse they can be unreasonable perfectionists.*

- *You know who I mean don't you? No matter __what__ you do for them it's never enough, or good enough, is it?*

We all know people who are **'sad'**:

- *They're glass half empty people who tend to notice and dwell on the negative news and incidents that happen to all of us at different times in our lives.*

- *Because of their perspective they see setbacks and tragedies as confirmation of their view of the problems and sadness of the world.*

We all know people who wallow in **'hurt'**:

- *They tend to be life's **'victims'**.*

- *They focus obsessively on the people and events they feel have damaged them, or robbed them. They use these events to feed and justify their behaviour.*

- *To them, the reasons for their problems are always outside of themselves; when things go wrong it's **never** their fault, they've always got an excuse!*

We all see and know people like these don't we, but what most of us don't realise is how often other people look at us and see the same sort of behaviour:

OUCH!

It's true. It's often obvious to other people that negative emotions are causing us problems... we just don't see it ourselves, because we're too close. The good news is we don't have to do lots of therapy to get better at this we just need to work on our self-esteem/self-image.

I mentioned earlier that **'limiting beliefs'** hold us back as well and as you'll see in a moment they nearly always go hand in hand with **negative emotions.**

The good news is beliefs don't have to be limiting, they can be empowering too.

I'm passionate about the idea that positive empowering beliefs are a vital tool in making it easy for you to **'DO'** something different in your salon today.

I truly **'believe'** our beliefs are the foundation of our results, and a poor self-image leads to limiting beliefs which in turn leads to negative and destructive behaviour!

Here's a question that will help you see the link between the three things.

Do you think people who are driven by anger, fear, guilt, sadness or hurt would **'believe'** it's:

- *OK to trust?*

- *OK to let go?*

- *OK to delegate?*

- *OK to look for the possibilities in every situation?*

- *OK to fail from time to time; and mistakes are simply lessons from which we can learn?*

NO!

So it follows that, because they don't **'believe'** these things, it's **IMPOSSIBLE** for them to do them! But here's the really important point: Successful leaders and managers **'DO'** believe them and **would 'DO'** them!

So, we all need to be prepared to work on our self image and self esteem and if you don't know where to start, you might like to try a Paul McKenna book called **'Change Your Life in 7**

Days'. Forget any images you may have about Paul McKenna and his stage shows and...

- *read the book*

- *do the simple exercises*

- *listen to the CD that comes FREE with the book every day for a month.*

If you do, I promise you'll find a **massive** difference: in the way you feel, the way you behave and the way people respond to you.

I remember how badly I needed help with my self-image before I could make my business work, so I **know** how important this is, but you must realise...

- *buying the book **isn't enough***

- *just reading the book **isn't enough***

- *you have to **take action***

- ***listen** to the CD daily*

- ***do** the exercises.*

Do all this and you'll find everything becomes possible.

By the way, reading and listening to Paul McKenna isn't the **only** way you can improve your 'self-image', it's just a low cost, *easy to fit into your life,* way to do it. If you'd like to explore the alternatives, look on Google using the search terms '**low self-esteem'**, or '**poor self-image'** and you'll find plenty to choose from.

Let's move on now to another important lesson.

To make change that lasts takes discipline.

Think about it...

- *You need **discipline** to buy the book I've just recommended*

- *You need **discipline** to read it*

- *You need **discipline** to listen to the CD*

- *You need **discipline** to do the exercises.*

For all these things you need **self-discipline.** But you're not the **only** one. If your business is going to grow, your team need to respond in a disciplined way as well and the cornerstone of discipline is a set of **rules.**

Why am I telling you this when it might appear obvious? Quite simply, it's because far too many salons don't have a clear set of rules. They **think** they do, but they're not written down and aren't applied consistently, which leads to all sorts of problems.

I'm not saying **'you'** have to write the rules without consulting your staff. If members of your team have the right attitude and suitable experience they absolutely **must** be involved in helping you create them. But once you've created the rules, everyone must sign to say they understand them and agree to stick to them.

By the way this applies to you too!

In his book **'The E Myth Revisited'** *(highly recommended)* the author **Michael E Gerber** makes the point that as the owner of the salon you have two different roles.

1. *Working 'on' your business: This means making strategic decisions to ensure it's got the investment, training and resources it needs to carry on growing.*

2. *Working 'in' your business: This means doing clients and carrying out your day to day leadership and management functions.*

Can you see the difference? Michael then goes on to say that when you're working **'in'** your business you absolutely **MUST** abide by the same rules and standards you expect your staff to work to.

Now you might find this hard to believe, but I've seen salon owners who don't allow staff to use mobile phones in the salon *keep their own phone with them while they're working on the floor.*

I've seen salon owners who quite rightly don't allow staff to drink coffee on the salon floor *keep a cup on the side for themselves, and think it's 'OK' because it's their salon.*

BUT IT'S NOT OK!

If you think you're **'above the law'** and that the rules don't apply to you when you're working alongside your staff, you're asking for trouble, **GREAT BIG HEAPS OF IT**, because you'll end up with an **'us and them'** culture!

If this is ringing bells for you, take a careful look at which of your salon rules you're breaking at the moment because you think it's **'OK'**!

I'm sure you've got the point, so let's move on.

Rules are great because they give everyone rights and **responsibilities.** They give you the chance to reward the people who stick to them, and make sure there are consequences for the people who break them. But there's something beyond rules we need to think about as well.

We need to think about **standards.**

What's the difference between a rule and a standard? Rules simply state what you can and can't do. Standards define how well something needs to be done. They are the next step and you'd better think about your standards carefully when you're creating your salon's rules.

You need to define an acceptable standard of performance from your stylists, covering things like...

- *how many clients they should do*

- *their average bill*

- *total sales*

- *retail sales*

- *client retention and so on.*

You need to define your acceptable standards of dress and etiquette, which would cover things like...

- *punctuality*
- *politeness*
- *consideration for the needs of others*
- *uniform or dress code*
- *standards of personal appearance and so on.*

You need to define your acceptable standards of attitude and we'll be looking at this in more detail later in the book.

You need to be very clear what the rewards are for those who meet and exceed your standards, and what the consequences are for those who don't!

You have to measure your team's performance and behaviour against your standards fairly and consistently, so you know what's happening.

Finally you have to act as an impartial referee and decide when a goal's been scored by your team and when a yellow or red card is needed!

FACT: If your 'self-image' is strong enough you'll find it easy to create and referee a fair and effective set of rules and standards.

FACT: If your 'self-image' is weak you'll struggle to create and referee a fair and effective set of rules and standards.

This is because, having a poor self-image creates a power vacuum, and with it an unwritten invitation for other people to come in and undermine everything you try and do. You literally, **but unknowingly**, invite people to give you a hard time!

- *Some salon owners try filling their vacuum and regaining control by nagging, or by being very strict.*

- *Others try and do it with **bribery** by giving extra attention, status, flattery, incentives, or money to the people who are undermining them and causing all the problems.*

- ***I also see them make the massive mistake of taking the good people around them for granted, just because they're not causing trouble!***

Do any of these strategies help?

No!

None of them get to the root of the problem, so while they may appear to have a short term effect, they don't work for long and they nearly always create more problems than they solve!

So **'DO'** work on improving your self-image first, **before** you try and make any other changes to your salon... you'll be glad you did!

CHAPTER 2

'DO' trust!

O K ... let's assume you've now boosted your self-esteem and got a rock solid self-image... What comes next?

Well now we have the internal confidence to trust **ourselves**, it becomes much easier to start trusting other people, and trust is the glue that's going to hold your salon together. Without it, you'll **NEVER** get done!'

Why is it so important? Because you have to trust before you can let go... **and failing to let go is a big mistake.**

Why?

Let me explain. When it comes to the discipline of managing our salons and leading our staff, most Salon Owners are **very** talented at doing certain things and that's good news, but no matter how talented any of us may be at doing some things, as human beings its inevitable we're only going to be **'average'** and way outside our comfort zone doing others!

Bear that in mind while we look at a list of the key areas which have to be well organised and run professionally if your salon is to thrive...

- *Marketing;*

- *Stock Control*
- *Accounts/Wages/Admin*
- *Health and safety*
- *Staff recruitment*
- *Staff training*
- *Staff motivation*
- *Artistic leadership*
- *Customer service*
- *Property maintenance*
- *Strategic planning.*

Can you agree they're **all** critical parts of your business, *(that's what I discovered as I developed my **"Do Something Different Success System"**)* and as the salon owner you're responsible for making sure your business does them **ALL** properly!

The important question is: "Which are you good at and which do you do badly, or ignore completely until a problem hits you **'SLAP'** right in the face?"

You need to answer this question, so go back to the list and look at it again with honesty. You must decide which activities play to your strengths and which bore you, frustrate you, or even scare you.

When you've finished going through the list you simply need to focus on two things.

1. *Actively taking responsibility for the areas that play to your strengths.*

2. *Finding a way to get the others done by people who are equipped to do them well... **In other words letting go and DELEGATING THEM!***

You're probably thinking, that sounds great Steve, **but I don't know how to DO it!**

The good news is, we've already covered the first **'DO'** step when we looked at building a positive self-image and high self-esteem. But here's something you need to understand.

FACT: People with a poor self-image find it very hard to trust and delegate effectively. People with a strong self-image do it <u>easily.</u>

FACT: If you don't learn to delegate you'll <u>never</u> grow your business beyond a certain limited size and you certainly won't be able to 'DO' the key things that are really going to make a difference today or any other day!

So now you probably realise what I meant when I said that your self-esteem and your ability to delegate are linked and you can't delegate effectively until you've got high self-esteem, although lots of salon owners try and then wonder why it doesn't work!

Here's another question for you to think about: Did you find it **'easy'** to go through that list of activities a few minutes ago and sort out what **'you'** should do and what you should delegate?

If you didn't, it's absolutely essential that you get to know yourself better, so you can play to your strengths in future.

To help you build a clearer picture of *'what you're naturally good at'* we're going to do a simple exercise taken from my *"Do Something Different Success System"*.

All you need to do is grab a pencil, read the following questions and write down your answers in the book.

Let's make a start.

- **Are you naturally tidy ... or untidy?**

I am _____

- **Which is more important to you security: or freedom?**

I think _____ *is more important*

- **Do you need 'to do' lists, wall planners and a personal organiser to function: or are you happier just writing things down on the nearest scrap of paper and filing stuff in piles?**

I prefer _____

- **Are you an 'always on time' person: or a 'just about on time' some of the time person.**

I am _____

- **Are you an 'ideas' person who spends lots of time day dreaming: or a people person who craves the company and contact of others all the time?**

I am _____

- *Are you good at starting things and then you get bored so most of them don't get finished: or are you determined to finish what you start, no matter what?*

I am _____

Have you answered every question? Has it helped you to see what you need some help with? I hope so, but let me see if I can make it even clearer for you!

A salon needs to be tidy.

Why?

Because at least 40% of the population are totally turned off by a dirty or untidy environment. **You can't afford to turn off that many people.** If being tidy doesn't come naturally to you, it will hold back the development of your business, so it makes sense to get someone who is **naturally** tidy to take responsibility!

The vast majority of your staff and clients crave the security of knowing where they stand, what they can expect and how they fit in. In other words, they like routine, they like structure and they like consistency.

If you love freedom and the flexibility to change your mind whenever you feel like it, you'll find it hard to communicate and deliver an experience that makes the people around you feel secure. The danger is they'll go somewhere else looking for security and your business won't grow.

So if you're very flexible by nature and freedom is more important than security, you'll be a weak link in the development of your salon. This means it makes sense to get someone who values security to organise you **and** manage your business to make sure your people are given the security they need!

A salon needs to be well organised with rules, systems and proper records. This helps everyone be clear about what's expected of them, helps you measure everyone's contribution consistently and it also protects **you** from unwanted problems if anything needs investigating in future.

If you're not a naturally organised person who's good at keeping records, planning for meetings and getting the right things done at the right time, you'll be a weak link in the development of your business. So get someone who's good at record keeping and running systems to do it for you!

A salon needs to run to a time schedule. If you're someone who finds this difficult, you'll be seen as unreliable, inconsistent and some people will find it hard to trust you. If other people's time isn't important to you, you'll be a weak link in the growth of your business, so give someone permission to manage your time for you and remind you where you have to be **and when!**

It's great to be creative and come up with good ideas that can take your business forward; but it's also important that your people feel cared for, appreciated and nurtured. Very few people can do both well, so do what you're good at and *get some help with the rest!*

It's great if you're good at starting things, but they need to be finished as well. Very few people can do both consistently, so do what you're good at and *get some help with the rest!*

Are you getting the message?

Very few of us are good at everything, but your business needs someone to be responsible for **everything** and it's an expensive mistake to be responsible for things we don't enjoy or take pride in doing well.

I recommend you keep learning about yourself because it gives you the knowledge you need to build on your known strengths and delegate round your weaknesses. Doing this gives you the freedom to take control of your business **and ignoring this fact is a very expensive mistake!**

By the way, I understand that some of this will be way outside your '**comfort zone**' and might seem a bit of a challenge, so if the thought of trusting others enough to delegate responsibility for any of the responsibilities I listed on page 38 seems a bit daunting, you might find my *"Do Something Different Success System"* which I've mentioned a couple of times, very helpful because it gives you all the tools and support you could need to create a well organised and profitable salon staffed by employees you can trust!

You'll find more details in the last chapter, so when you're ready, have a look.

CHAPTER 3

'DO' choose!

So far the focus of this book has been you, but in this chapter we're going to give you a break by looking at the people you have around you instead and look more closely at what you can 'DO' to choose between those who are obviously good for your business and those who you might **think** are... **but are actually causing most of your problems!**

With that understood let's start learning more about the powerful positive benefits of making the right choices by checking your current staff using a simple exercise from my *"Do Something Different Success"* system.

Get a piece of paper and make a list of the names of everyone you employ, or who's involved in any way with helping you run your salon.

When you've done that, take each name on your list in turn, and based on your experience of working with them, ask yourself the following **4** questions ... *(Go with your gut reaction when you're doing this exercise and take no more than 5 seconds to answer any of the questions.)*

Question 1.

Does this person have an attitude I'm comfortable with, and

the skills to do the job I want?

YES or NO

Question 2.

Does this person have an attitude I'm comfortable with, but their skills need improving to get to the right level?

YES or NO

Question 3.

Does this person have an attitude I find frustrating and challenging but has the skills needed to do the job well?

YES or NO

Question 4.

Does this person have an attitude I find frustrating and challenging, and their skills need improving to get to the right level?

YES or NO

Each time you ask this series of questions, the person concerned should end up with **3 'No's'** and **1 'Yes'** as answers, and all I want you to do is make a note of the **number** of the question you answered **'Yes'** to, next to their name on the list.

When you do this exercise properly you should finish with a list of names, and next to each name will be the number of the question you answered 'YES' to. Is that what you've got?

If it is, then what shall we do with the information?

Ask yourself, who deserves your time, energy, support and encouragement:

- *The people who are supporting you and have an attitude you can work with?*

- *Or the people who frustrate you, and want to pull you in different directions to suit their own agenda?*

The answer is obvious isn't it! You have to discriminate and choose to work with those that want to work with **you** and they're the people who've got a number 1 or number 2 next to their name on your list.

What's not so obvious and why the ability to see the difference is so important is this; instead of trying to bribe or motivate your 'number 3s and 4s' to change their behaviour... ***just do 2 things:***

1. *Every time they fail to meet a standard, ignore a system, break a rule or cause a problem, take them to one side and in a quiet, non-emotional, **professional** manner, tell them what they've done wrong, explain it's unacceptable and be very clear what the consequences will be if they do it again.*

2. *Every time they do something positive that you want to encourage, **pay them the compliment of noticing and saying well done.***

The rest of the time you simply **ignore** them except for the usual day to day need to be polite and professional because it's not your job to **'rescue'** them!

FACT: Only someone with a positive self-image will be able to do this consistently, but if you do manage it, one of <u>two</u> things will happen very quickly:

1. *They'll get fed up because their tactics aren't working anymore and leave.*

2. *They'll modify their behaviour to get more of the praise they now deserve and you won't want them to leave!*

Either way you win!

Ignoring **'the number 3 lesson'** will not only cost you a lot of money but years of frustration and heartache as well!

Once you've made sure your current team is number 3 and 4 free, your next job is to make sure you never take on any more in future which makes your interviewing process **critically important,** so that's what we'll talk about next.

To achieve a team free of number 3's and 4's we need to interview in a way that makes sure we get a clear picture of the self-image, beliefs, values and attitude of the person we're thinking of employing, ***before we offer them a job.***

To help you, here are a set of interviewing rules from my ***"Do Something Different Success System"*** that have served countless salon owners very well!

Before I get to the specific rules here are four guiding principles to follow:

1. **Conduct your interviews in the 'right' frame of mind:** It's so important not to be desperate. One of my favourite sayings is: **"It's better to have <u>no</u> staff than the wrong staff."**

2. **Hire slowly and fire <u>quickly</u>:** Take the time to interview candidates thoroughly, then give your staff the chance to meet them and express an opinion as well, before you finally decide whether to offer a 3 month trial period or not... **and if you have any doubts or concerns during those first 3 months, take that as a sign, let them go and be prepared to start again.**

3. **Don't take <u>anything</u> you're told during an interview at face value:** Use it as a starting point for further discussion... **and that's it!**

4. **Know what you're looking for:** You must understand that getting a feeling for a candidate's self-image, attitudes, beliefs and values is <u>**far**</u> more important to you than a picture of their current skill level: This is simply because it's much easier to train the 'right' person to become a good hairdresser... **than it is to train a good hairdresser to become the 'right' person for your team.**

Follow these principles and you won't go far wrong.

Now let's move on to the rules of interviewing I promised you:

1. *Start with a suitable venue that sets the right tone. Don't use your staff room or anywhere that you can be interrupted.*

2. *If you don't have a suitable place in your salon, use a local*

coffee shop. I've held many interviews at **Costa Coffee** *for example and I've found if you buy tea or coffee at regular intervals they're quite happy for you to be there.*

3. *How and where you sit is important; so to help you get your body language right, sit at the same level as the person you're interviewing with no barriers between you and preferably at a 90 degree angle to them.*

4. *Start the interview with a brief scene setting speech, which makes lots of points that they would naturally agree with and nod a couple of times every few seconds while you're saying it to promote agreement and help relax your candidate.*

5. *Remember, while we're interviewing, what we're* **really** *looking to discover are the beliefs, attitudes and values that make them* **'who'** *they are.*

6. *The secret to doing this is to* **'listen carefully'** *for things they say that don't add up or feel right, things that make you curious, things they seem to get emotional about, things that reveal their attitudes and beliefs. When you hear any of these things, follow up a.s.a.p. by asking perceptive questions…* **and then keep your mouth firmly 'SHUT' and listen while they talk!**

By the way, it may help if you follow a simple rule, which is: **never, Never, NEVER** *think about what you're going to say next* **while** *a candidate is talking. If you do,* **you're** **not** **listening** *and you might miss something important … Instead just pay attention to what's being said and* **how** *it's being said until they've finished talking, you'll be surprised what you notice!"*

When they stop, just pause for a moment and reflect on what you've heard then pick up on whatever caught your attention and either ask them to tell you more about it, or flip their statement into a question.

To give you an example of flipping a statement into a question, they might say that they **'hated'** being at school.

You could flip that by saying: "You said you **'hated'** school, I'm curious, what happened to make you feel like that?"

Remember, reflecting language and even their gestures back to an interviewee if they get emotional about something, will give them the feeling you understand them deeply.

This means they are far more likely to open up and tell you more. In fact, when you learn to reflect well, *you'll get to know them much better than they really want you too!*

Now, let's get back to the interview structure. If after you've had your chat you're pretty sure the person isn't who you're looking for, simply thank them for coming and tell them you'll write and let them know your decision when you've finished interviewing.

If you think they have potential, pay them the compliment of saying so, and then ask: "What questions would you like to ask me?"

As you answer their questions, look for the right time to give them a clear picture of what they can expect if they're successful.

For example I'm always looking for the right opportunity to say:

> *"You must understand I'm not looking for someone who simply wants a job; I'm looking for someone who wants a **career.***
>
> *If you're successful and join us you'll be given the opportunity, the tools and the environment to create a successful career, but, and it's a **BIG BUT,** whether you achieve it or not is up to **you.***
>
> *Of course the team and I will be here to guide and help you, but we can't and **won't** do it for you; and if we **ever** get the feeling you're not committed to making the most of the opportunity, we'll be parting company: **now, do you still want to join us?"***

Do you know what? If candidate gets this far, they always say **YES!** So ask yourself: "What would my version of that speech sound like... what do they **'really'** need to know about working with us?"

The final step I suggest you follow in the interviewing process is another simple exercise from my *"**Do Something Different Success** System."*

Give them 4 sheets of paper. Each one should have one of the following symbols on it.

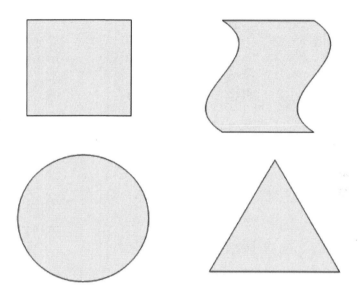

Ask them to put the sheets in order, with their favourite on the top, their second favourite next and so on. You'll find the **'order'** they choose tells you a lot about their priorities and what makes them tick.

But here's a word of warning.

This exercise is only about **80%** accurate, so <u>do</u> check your results by following up their selection with extra questions. I find the best way to check is to ask if they've ever done this exercise before, *which they rarely* have and then ask if they'd like you to explain what it all means: ***they always say yes!***

Then I tell them about the typical characteristics of the type of people who prefer each symbol, which are ***as follows.***

People who choose the square first normally:

- *Love detail.*

- *Make lists.*

- *Hate being late.*

- *Always tidy up and put things away after they've finish using them.*

People who choose the circle first normally:

- *Love people.*

- *Enjoy entertaining them.*

- *Like caring for them.*

- *Only feel complete when they're in the company of other people.*

People who choose the squiggle first normally:

- *Love change.*

- *Hate being tied down.*

- *Are always changing their minds.*

- *Are often late.*

- *Are disorganised and untidy.*

- *But they do come up with great ideas!*

People who choose the triangle first normally:

- *Are driven to get things done.*

- *Get to the point.*

- *Are direct.*

- *Are focussed.*

- *Are competitive.*

- *Often don't care if they upset people.*

I tell them that most of us are a **'combination'** of characteristics from 2 and sometimes 3 of the shapes; but we all have a dominant way of behaving. I then explain what the order of their choice suggests to me about **them** ... and you'll notice from their reaction whether what you've said is true or not.

You can really have fun with this, because it doesn't matter whether what you've said is true or not! Why not? Because; either way, you'll find you can build on their reaction with your **'reflection'** technique and when you do, you'll discover more about what really makes them tick!

Just remember it doesn't matter which way you get to know them better, all that matters is *you do get to know them better!*

When you've finished you then have to decide if they're good enough to go on to the next stage of your hiring process.

For me, the next stage should always involve meeting and spending time with your team, so they can be part of the decision making process as well. If your candidate is going on to the next stage, let them know when they can expect to hear from you.

Hiring the wrong people can be VERY costly. Having read this chapter there's no excuse for doing the 'same old, same old' interviews anymore... is there!

CHAPTER 4

'DO' measure!

It's time to stop talking about people and start talking about the business of **'business'** but I promise I'll keep it simple, to the point and jargon free!

In this chapter, we're going to focus on what we need to measure and how we can use the information we've measured.

Measuring things doesn't sound sexy, does it, but think about it this way. How will you ever know if what you're **'DOING'** is working if you don't measure?

The good news is, done right, **'measurement' can become a very powerful motivation tool.**

The bad news is, far too many salon owners **don't** do it right and that's either because they're **'data nerds'** who eat, sleep and orgasm over data, or more commonly they are **'data phobics'** people who get overwhelmed by figures and end up avoiding them as much as they can.

Both types of salon owner are at risk of being a nightmare to work for, often ending up with demotivated staff who are either confused by data overload, or switched off because they don't get much data based feedback about how well they are doing.

This means what we're looking for is a healthy balance and that's what I aim to give you.

Now that's understood, what shall we measure first?

Let's start by saying that salon owners often give a lot of thought to their prices but rarely pay the same attention to measuring the time they allocate for a service relative to the price they charge and this can be an expensive mistake.

Let me show you why.

I was in a salon recently and I looked at their price list. **Children's cuts were £10** and they booked out 20 minutes for them. Their **Full Head Woven Highlights plus C/BD was £110** and 105 minutes were booked out for them.

Now imagine this salon owner had two stylists **WHO WERE BOTH FULLY BOOKED**, one doing children's cuts and the other doing full head woven highlights plus C/BD for a week. If it was a 39hour week the difference in turnover for the two stylists would be

- *Children's cuts turnover... £1170.00 which equates to £30 per hour.*

- *Full head highlights turnover... £2457.00 which equates to £63 per hour.*

The difference in revenue between £30 per hour and £63 per hour adds up to £1287 over a whole week and that difference is huge.

So the first thing I want you to **'DO'** different when it comes to measuring in future is to focus a lot more attention on **Revenue Per Hour.**

You need to measure:

- *The* **Revenue Per Hour** *generated by each of your stylists.*

- *The* **Revenue Per Hour** *potential of each of your services.*

Let's start with your stylists. All the research shows if you give people three or more targets at a time they can feel **over measured, unfairly judged, pressurised, stressed and ultimately,** they lose focus and end up achieving <u>less</u> ... **not more.**

This means to avoid these problems you'd have to give them targets on no more than <u>two</u> items from a quite a long list of possible candidates like...

- *their turnover*

- *their average bill*

- *their retail sales*

- *their technical services*

- *their rebooking rate*

- *their client retention rate*

- *their time utilisation.*

The bad news for you is, if you only focus on two targets, many opportunities could be missed.

The good news is giving them just one **Revenue Per Hour** based target gets around the problem.

How?

Because everything on the list above has an impact on their **Revenue Per Hour** and as long as a stylist is achieving their revenue per hour target, you're getting the result you want so you don't need to worry what they choose to focus on!

In other words, you're telling them what they need to achieve by setting an **Revenue Per Hour** target, but you're leaving it to them, *with some coaching from you if they want it,* to decide and implement **how** to achieve it.

Effectively you're giving them control and that's one of the most motivating things you give to anyone.

If you're wondering what **Revenue Per Hour** target you should set for your stylists, I'd suggest from experience it should be a **minimum of 4 times their basic hourly wage**, but remember this is just a minimum acceptable standard.

For team members to **earn** a promotion, a pay rise or large incentives or bonus I'd set them a target of **at least 5 times their basic pay and they'd have to achieve it over a 13 week period.**

So, to give you an example I'd suggest someone on **£7.50 per hour** would need to generate an average **£30 R.P.H.** as a

minimum acceptable standard and an average of **£37.50 per hour** over 13 weeks to earn a big reward.

Here's a simple formula from my *"Do Something Different Success System"* you can use to calculate a stylist's **Revenue Per Hour.**

Turnover ÷ Hours available for appointments = R.P.H.

I say hours available for appointments because it wouldn't be fair to penalise them for training time or attending meetings would it,

Next let's look at calculating **Revenue Per Hour** for services. It's important because very few salon owners create their price list with revenue per hour in mind. Instead they look at their competitors' prices and work round that, don't they.

This is a **dangerous** thing to do because, without realising it, you can easily create a price list riddled with low revenue per hour services that cripple your businesses ability to grow and be profitable.

Here's how to find out how badly you're affected.

Start by getting a paper copy of your price list.

Next to the price of every service on it I want you to write the number of minutes you book out for the service.

Finally get a calculator and go down your price list dividing the cost of every service by the number of minutes you book out and write the pence per minute next to each price then multiply it by 60 (minutes) to get the revenue per hour.

Just to be clear the formula is:

Price ÷ Minutes Booked Out x 60 = Revenue Per Hour.

You'll remember from the example we looked at a couple of pages ago that the **Revenue Per Hour** for different services can vary wildly so what should the minimum be when you go through or are creating your price list?

I'd recommend a minimum of 6 times the hourly basic rate of the lowest paid stylist providing the service.

So, to give you an example, if a stylist is **£7.50 per hour** the formula would be

£7.50 x 6 = £45 as the Minimum Revenue Per Hour acceptable for that service.

Remember this would be the **minimum** you should accept for a service on your price list but if the market will stand it, it's OK to go much, much higher!

If, after doing the exercise you find you have a service that's currently giving a lower revenue per hour figure than is ideal, then you need to do one of the following.

- *Reduce the time you mark out for the service to increase its revenue per hour.*

- *Increase the price to the minimum level needed.*

- *Discontinue the service.*

Most salon owners would find none of these options

comfortable and in my experience, if pushed to choose one they'd start making excuses rather than adopt any of them.

The blunt truth is by avoiding change all they are doing is crippling the ability of their stylists to earn fair rewards for what they do and also crippling the long-term development of their business.

By the way, in case you haven't worked it out yet, the fastest way for you or any of your stylists to drive their revenue per hour figures through the roof is by selling retail.

Why retail?

Because its **extra revenue for no extra time**... it's that simple and it proves beyond doubt that taking retail far more seriously than they currently do is an essential **'DO SOMETHING DIFFERENT PRIORITY'** for the vast majority of salon owners reading this book!

Now I want to move on to measuring **PROFIT.**

Profit is a slippery customer. We can't survive without it, but most of us learn the hard way that making a profit consistently isn't the easiest thing to do.

The main reason salon owners struggle is simply because they don't measure their profit until after the end of their financial year... **and by then it's too late to do anything about it.**

Instead they measure **turnover**, because they believe that creating a healthy turnover is the key to success.

It's an easy mistake to make, but it is a mistake, because it's only part of the story.

To consistently make a profit a business should set budgets for spending as well as measuring turnover.

Before we look at setting budgets in detail, there's something else you need to be aware of that has a dramatic effect on your ability to budget and I'm talking about 'The VAT Trap'.

'The VAT Trap' is the dramatic drop in profits a salon suffers when it registers for VAT and starts giving the government 13 pence in every pound of their turnover.

Do the sums and you'll discover that a salons turnover has to almost double before profits begin to grow again, which makes it almost impossible for salon owners to invest in the growth needed to recoup the lost profits and go on to grow a large healthy long-lasting business. This has led to 'VAT Trap' avoidance on a large scale which is distorting our industry to such an extent that under 10% of the salons in the UK are growing healthily.

'VAT Trap' avoidance means:

- *Few salons are investing in ongoing training, because there's no point.*

- *Very few salons now offer an inspiring career path to attract young people into the industry and keep them there happily for twenty or thirty years.*

- *The young people who do come into our industry are trained mainly at their local college and struggle to find jobs once they are qualified.*

- *Recently qualified stylists who do find jobs struggle to build busy columns.*

- *Busy stylists with full columns are tempted to leave employed positions by the lure of earning more money for less work renting a chair.*

I could go on, but the simple fact is that for all these reasons and many more, **'VAT Trap'** avoidance is draining our industry of its lifeblood and its future.

Change may be on the horizon however because the chancellor has commissioned a report looking into how the current VAT structure is affecting small businesses, which some experts are suggesting may lead to a dramatic reduction in the VAT threshold.

If this happens it will trigger big changes in our industry. With changes like these comes opportunity for some salon owners and stressful problems for others.

The cool fact is, you get to choose whether it would be an opportunity or problem for you because if you follow the guidelines I give you in this book you'll automatically end up in the opportunity camp as your salon thrives and grows stronger year after year.

Assuming you are, or intend to be a salon that thrives both before **and** after any VAT changes let's look at how you can budget to keep control of your spending.

I've already told you that the UK Government will take 13p

out of every pound away from you before you even start paying your bills, so you need to budget for that.

This will leave you 87 pence in every pound left. *(In case you're wondering why it's not 20 pence it's because the government allow you to claim about 7 pence back, leaving you 13 pence out of pocket.)*

Next you should budget for making a profit of 20p out of every pound.

Very few salon owners budget for profit, instead they cross their fingers and hope, so if you truly are going to **'DO something different in your salon today'** setting a budget for profit would be a great thing way to start!

Now if you've been counting, you'll know that once VAT and your profit have been put to one side you've only got 67 pence in every pound left to pay for **everything** else.

As VAT and your profit are non-negotiable how you spend your 67 pence in every pound is where you should put your budgeting focus and in my *"Do Something Different Success System"* I have a **Quarterly Budget Sheet** that makes planning your profit so much easier… **and if you'd like a copy I'll tell you how you can get one for free at the end of the book.**

Even without the budget sheet you can do a lot to help you see the whole picture more clearly, here's a brief breakdown of the general guidelines I give salon owners to help them spend the 67 pence in the pound wisely:

- *Your biggest expense is staff and I recommend you budget to spend 40 pence in the pound or less including your own wages and the wages of your support staff.*

- *The next on the list is stock and I recommend you budget to spend 14 pence in the pound or less on this, including your retail stock.*

- *Next comes Rent and rates and I recommend you budget to spend 5 pence in the pound or less on this.*

- *Finally, everything else: Marketing, training, heat and light, telephone, refreshments etc and If you've been doing your sums you'll know there are only **8** pence in the pound left to pay for all these, so spend your money wisely!*

Here's a diagram to help you see it more clearly.

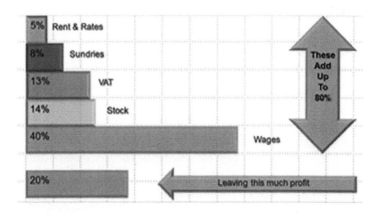

As you've just seen, your wages bill is your biggest expense so your staff performance needs to be measured constantly.

The easiest way to do it is with a Point Of Sale computer system which measures the performance of your whole business. I couldn't imagine running a salon without one. Any time I want to check anything it only takes a couple of minutes... **brilliant!**

I'm often asked which system and software I'd recommend and my answer is... **Shortcuts.** I've used it for years. I've found it accurate, reliable, good value for money and the support I've had from them has been excellent!

With that said, let's get back to your wages bill and I've already given you one of the biggest secrets to getting value for money for the wages you pay and that's setting targets based on Revenue Per Hour **and** building your reward structure around achieving those targets.

Since I implemented a wage structure based on Revenue Per Hour in my *"Do Something Different Success System"* I have never been asked for a pay rise by my stylists.

Why?

Because as I told you earlier, their performance is measured against a **13 week target** and if they hit it they automatically get a pay rise and often promotion as well!

Now 13 weeks is a long time to expect a stylist to keep their focus, so I have regular one to one appraisals with each stylist where I help build their confidence and belief and coach them on how to improve so they achieve their goals.

The combination of 13 week targets, with automatic pay rises, and regular meetings is very powerful and motivating… **and this is proved by the fact that it's not unusual for a stylist to earn more than one pay rise a year.**

You may be thinking; **"I couldn't afford anything like that Steve"** but the answer is, if stylists are busy and profitable for the salon, then of course you can afford it!

By the way, another question I'm often asked is how much time do I give stylists to start hitting target if they've just qualified, or have joined me from another salon.

My answer is this. If a stylist is recently qualified I give them a year to start hitting the full minimum target of 4 x times basic wage. If they join me from another salon with no clients they get 6 months to start hitting it. If they join me from another salon with clients they get 3 months.

Giving people time to grow is all very well, but you have to realise there's a massive difference between how you should treat someone who's actively growing their turnover and will soon reach target and someone who's hit a plateau level and isn't making progress.

The **'grower'** will respond to towards motivation because they can see what they are aiming for, believe they can do it and they want to get there. For them encouragement and rewards will work well.

The **'sticker'** by contrast is someone who has probably reached their natural level and if you leave them alone, that's where they'll stay. Plodding along, costing you money. **More fool you if you accept that situation, or believe there's nothing you can do about it.**

These people need away motivation. You need to turn the comfort zone where they are living into a **'discomfort zone'** by using your regular meetings to explain in calm non-judgemental language that their current level of performance is below the standards required and if it continues... **their employment won't!**

Be fair. Give them an achievable goal and a reasonable amount of time to achieve it.

Measure their progress and have weekly meetings if needed. Praise progress but be prepared to carry out your threat if they don't reach target by the deadline... **don't make the mistake many salon owners make of letting things drift.**

By the way I'm not a lawyer and I don't do legal advice. The process I've just described is, as far as I'm aware, legal in the UK as long as you are clear, consistent and fair with your staff.

If I were you though I'd belong to an organisation like the **National Hairdressers Federation** which provides free legal advice and indemnity as part of their membership package.

As a member, whenever you have a problem you can make a quick phone call before following the **exact** instructions you're given. Do this and should the problem end up **'going legal'** further down the line, you're covered.

If you remember, after wages, the next biggest expense you have as a salon owner is stock.

I've always believed that it's better to build a strong relationship with one supplier rather than spreading my business around.

To prove I practice what I preach I have had a very successful 21-year relationship with **Goldwell/KMS**

By committing to spend my stock budget with them I can access the best discounts possible.

Saving money is all very well *(it certainly helps me with budgeting)* but it's actually **more** important that my staff love their products and the training and marketing support they provide free of charge is always consistent and of a high quality.

In all the strong relationship between us has played a large part in creating a very strong colour business... **and our KMS retail sales have grown by 550% in the last four years as well!**

There are also motivation tools provided like **Goldwell's Colorzoom** which is an international colour competition with finals held in a different amazing location each year.

The motivation to qualify for a place on the **Colorzoom** trip really drives the performance of a number of my team members.

Always remember that by definition a relationship is a two-way street which means when partnering with a company like **Goldwell** you have to play your part and use the tools and support they provide.

You'd be amazed how many salon owners, don't send their staff on courses, don't use the marketing tools, don't engage in the promotions and competitions… **and then moan because nothing is changing for them!**

Now we've covered the two main areas where spending can get out of control, but if you'd like more help with budgeting and the DIY approach of using my Quarterly Budget Sheet doesn't appeal I recommend you get in touch with **Chris Cheeney** from **CDC accounting** *(look them up on Google)* because he specialises in helping salon owners control their costs and manage their cashflow.

He looks after the financial affairs of salon owners all over the country *(including mine)* and the good news is that unlike most accountants he **really** understands what makes us salon owners tick… **because he and his wife run one of the most profitable beauty salons in the country!**

Now moving on from measuring staff performance and salon running costs it will also pay us to understand there's something useful we can **'DO'** to measure our clients as well.

We can **'DO'** it by using the report that shows you top 500 clients, by spend, in the last year.

If you plotted how much the 500 spend in a year on a graph you'd notice a typical pattern showing a relatively small group of clients at the top who are your **'Big Spenders'.**

Next you'd notice the graph beginning to drop as the spending drops but the number who are still spending quite a lot grows significantly. Let's call this larger group your **'Bread and Butter Spenders.'**

Finally you'd see the biggest group of all are the clients who spend the least and we'll call them your **'Poor Spenders.'**

Now, here's a question that should be easy to answer. Which group of **'Spenders'** do you want more of in your salon?

Of course, it's the **'Big Spenders'.**

Bearing that in mind the important question to ask yourself is, should you treat all your clients the same, or should your 'Big Spenders' be recognized and treated differently?

Of course you should make a fuss of and recognise your best customers. Give them flowers from time to time, hold an annual party for them, or take them out to dinner. Invite them to focus groups and listen to what they have to say. Give them a proper V.I.P. club to belong to. Do whatever it takes.

Why?

Because you're far less likely to lose them if you show you appreciate them, aren't you and they are bringing you the majority of your profits!

There's another benefit as well. If you make your fuss publicly, other clients will know what you're doing and why and some of them will want to join in and the only way they can do that is to spend more, which is exactly what you want.

To sum it up, following the **'make a bigger fuss of your best clients'** policy achieves two things:

1. *Your big spenders stay loyal for longer.*

2. *Your average spenders aspire to join the big spender group.*

Either way your profits go up.

CHAPTER 5

'DO' communicate clearly!

As salon owners, we all know we **need** to communicate clearly, but most of us don't truly understand what it is and how to do it effectively.

The first key point I want to get across is that communicating clearly is the secret to dramatically improving the marketing of your salon.

It's true.

Many of us think marketing is about special offers, promotions and advertising; and it is, partly!

But it's also more, a **lot** more.

It's about:

- *Everything that makes our salons **interesting** to potential clients.*

- *Anything that gets us **noticed** and talked about.*

- *Anything that makes us **exciting, attractive or worthy of comment**.*

- *Anything that creates **'word of mouth'**, or **'word of media'** interest.*

I wonder what people say about your salon?

What do you give them to talk about?

I hope its lots of:

- *Positive news.*

- *Great offers.*

- *Professional advice.*

- *Education.*

I hope it's not about:

- *The state of your toilets.*

- *The stains on your towels.*

- *The fact that your staff don't seem to care, because they're too busy gossiping or falling out with each other to pay much attention to anyone else!*

I hope it's not about the time:

- *They were kept waiting.*

- *They were overcharged.*

- *Your drains smelled awful.*

- *Your new receptionist ignored them while she chatted on the phone to a friend!*

Give them half a chance and most clients are more than

happy to revel in gossiping and moaning about the bad stuff that happens, no matter how **good** your haircuts are!

We must never forget there's always someone waiting to re-interpret anything that happens in your salon to make it more gossip worthy. So the question I want you to think about is how can you **'Do Clear Communication'** and take control of the 'News' agenda of your salon?

Remember if you don't, **others** will do it for you. The first thing to **'DO'** is go back and check that your salon really is clean, tidy, well organised and that it runs to time. You must understand that this is a very important part of clear communication.

The next thing to **'DO'** is make sure you've got a great atmosphere.

How do you make sure the atmosphere's great? By realising you live in a world that's become very detached and impersonal. This knowledge gives you the perfect opportunity to stand out from the crowd and make clients feel important and cared for.

Here are some tips to help you and your staff to deliver a great salon atmosphere:

- *Smile genuinely. When you make eye contact with every client and smile. You'll see them smile back.*

- *Give sincere compliments. Stop focussing on yourself and pay every client two or three sincere compliments. It shows you care.*

- **Use your client's name.** Remember, the sweetest sound is someone's own name. Find out what they like to be called and try using it 4 or 5 times during an appointment.

- **Make regular eye contact.** Make sure you look directly into your client's eyes when they talk to you. This will show them you're interested.

- **Use humour.** It's OK to be playful and get silly sometimes. Don't be afraid to laugh, it's infectious.

- **Never argue with a client.** You can never <u>ever</u> win in the long run, even if a client is wrong! Remember this isn't a game and we're not fighting a war either, we're running a business.

- **If there's a problem, keep calm.** Don't get dragged into the drama or emotional tension a problem can create.

- **Fix the experience.** Remember, if a client is unhappy it's not enough to fix the problem, you have to fix the <u>experience.</u> It's how they feel afterwards that matters.

Please don't ignore these tips. They may be simple but they are priceless.

If you make the mistake of taking your clients for granted you'll regret it in the end.

As I said earlier you have to focus on getting the basic experience right first.

Then and **only** then, when you're sure you can really deliver on the promises you make, is it safe to start communicating your marketing.

Spending money on advertising and promotions when the basic experience you're offering isn't right is a **very** expensive mistake. It means you're spending money attracting people to your business just to show them you've got problems!

Very clever... NOT!

But let's assume you've got the basics right, what comes next in your clear communication strategy?

A salon newsletter would be a great place to start. Combine it with a lively, fun, interactive social media strategy and a membership club with special perks for your clients and you'll be well set.

If you're not sure what to say in your newsletter or on social media, you need to learn how to make things 'newsworthy'.

Have a look in some newspapers, magazines, or on the web and you'll see what the professionals do to grab your attention.

They focus on things that are:

- *The first.*

- *The latest.*

- *The oldest.*

- *The biggest.*

- *The smallest.*

- *New.*

- *Improved.*

- *An anniversary celebration.*

- *Award winning;.*

I could go on!

To create news, you can also:

- *Give your opinion on something that's making the news. For example, long before her 'is she isn't she' having a baby dominated the tabloid press, Cheryl Cole was in the news for promoting a L'Oreal shampoo that gave volume and bounce... when in fact she wearing hair extensions! You could have commented on news like that couldn't you!*

- *Give something away **FREE**. (More on this later!)*

- *Hold a survey, or comment on the results of a survey.*

- *Support a charity.*

- *Solve a problem for your clients.*

- *Attempt to beat or set a record.*

- *Create a publicity stunt based on characters in a hit film.*

By the way, half the battle in making your communication clearly newsworthy is creating a great headline, because the headline is the 'marketing' for the 'marketing'!

If it doesn't attract your audience's attention, it doesn't matter how good the rest of your communication is, it won't be read.

Here's a simple tip that will help you create a never ending stream of fantastic headlines:

- *Grab some copies of the popular magazines that are bound to be available in your salon.*

- *Next, write a list of all the headlines you see on the front covers on a piece of paper.*

- *Then you can go down the list and adapt the best ones to fit whatever it is you're talking about!*

To show you how easy this is to do, I've just picked up a copy of Good Housekeeping. Here's a list of the headlines on the front cover:

- **10 Feel good ways to afford the life you want!**

- **What's normal and what's not? The no panic guide to your health.**

- **Transform yourself... "We changed our looks and our lives."**

- **Get more energy naturally and protect your immunity too.**

Let's play with these and see how you could adapt them to communicate clearly in your salon newsletter, on your website and on social media.

How about:

- **10 Feel good styles you can afford to wear!**

- *What's normal and what's not? The no panic guide to unexpected hair loss!*

- *Transform your hair... transform your life!*

- *Give your hair more energy and bounce by following these 7 simple tips!*

Do you see what I mean?

It's an easy way of coming up with attention grabbing headlines and an easy way to get ideas for interesting articles you can write as well.

Now if I can do this with headlines from a magazine that's as mundane as Good Housekeeping what could you do with the headlines from something far punchier like Cosmo!!!

Here's another tip that will help you make your communication much more 'newsworthy'.

Collect testimonials and stories of positive experiences from your clients and use them wherever you can, to clearly communicate your message.

Remember that salon software like **Shortcuts** can automatically push client testimonials to your website and social media making it easy to keep your testimonials up to date.

Why are testimonials and client stories such a good idea?

Simply because if **you** say something… in the back of your clients mind you're selling, no matter how nicely you do it. But if another client says something or if it's a story about another client's experience, its interesting **NEWS!**

Remember, if there's always something new, different or exciting going on it will give your clients positive things to talk about… **which has got to be good news!**

But there's more to clear communication than just making sure what you do is newsworthy.

Here are 6 secrets that will help you do a really great job communicating clearly.

Secret Number 1.

Create a comprehensive salon database.

As an absolute minimum you must have on record, the first name, surname, address, mobile phone number and e mail address of EVERY CLIENT who comes into your salon.

Any salon that doesn't have an accurate, up to date client database is throwing away money.

Here are 3 very good reasons why you should do it.

Reason 1.

You can use appointment reminders to save you money and put a stop to no shows.

There's no excuse not to either because today, with systems

like Shortcuts, it's incredibly easy to automate the process and regularly send appointment reminders by text or email.

The good thing about appointment reminders is they show your clients you're professional, you care and you take your time seriously.

It stands to reason that if **you** communicate clearly that you take your time seriously... **your clients are more likely to do it as well, aren't they!**

Reason 2.

You can use **'we've missed you letters'** to bring back some of the clients you've **'lost'.**

Research has shown you lose clients for one of 4 reasons:

1. *They died.*

2. *They moved away.*

3. *You did something wrong, either a technical mistake or you took them for granted.*

4. *Something in their life interrupted them and they got out of the habit.*

You can't do anything about reasons 1 and 2 but you certainly can with numbers 3 and 4.

- *The first step is to know it's happening and your salon computer system will do that for you.*

- *The second step is to get in contact and genuinely ask them if they're alright.*

By the way if you're going to contact them, research has shown that a personalised **"we've missed you" letter** is much better than the mass produced **'come back'** leaflet or voucher many salons use.

Try following these simple steps when writing your letter:

- *Tell them you've noticed they don't come in any more.*

- *Say you hope they're alright and that you're concerned about them.*

- *Tell them in a caring way that you want to make sure that you didn't do anything wrong.*

- *Tell them if you or your team **did** do something wrong, you'll be happy to do whatever it takes to make it right again.*

- *Finally, make them an offer they can't refuse.*

What I've found since we've been using letters like this in my salon is that reason number 4, something in their life interrupted them and they got out of the habit, is the most common.

The fact that we've cared enough to write is enough to bring them back. Remember, every client you 'save' is like winning a new client, so once you get them back don't take them for granted.

Reason 3.

You can say **'Thank You'** which makes clients feel special.

One of the best times to start saying thank you to a client is a few days after their first appointment.

Did you know that new clients are 8 times more likely to become regular clients if they get past their 3rd appointment?

To me, that information suggests a thank you letter to encourage them would be a great way to communicate clearly that you care, wouldn't it!

But it's only the beginning. There are many great ways to say 'thank you' to clients. Why not see how many other ways you and your team can come up with.

So, now you know how important it is to have every client's details on record, what's the best way to collect them?

It's simple… set up a membership program.

When people join, ask them for:

- *First Name.*
- *Surname.*
- *Mobile number.*
- *E Mail Address.*
- *Home Address.*
- *Home Phone number.*

Now we can:

- *Remind them about their next appointment.*

- *Send them their **'recommend a friend'** rewards.*

- *Send them their monthly newsletter.*

- *Invite them to the **VIP Client Evenings**.*

- *Let them know about the next **VIP pamper days.***

- *Tell them about the special offers we've arranged for them from other local businesses.*

Can you see why clients are happy to give us their details! Can you see why a client database gives you the ability to take control of your business?

Secret Number 2.

Communicate clearly with your clients **regularly.**

Why?

Because we're in a competitive industry.

Do you realise that every day your competitors are trying to steal **your** clients?

I'm forever hearing about the dirty tricks that some salon owners get up to in a bid to steal clients from a competitors salon!

What can you do to tackle problems like this? The only thing that really works in the long run is making sure your clients know you care.

What makes the difference between a client who knows you care and one who doesn't?

Clear communication!

You already have a relationship with your existing clients, and your competitors don't, **YET**, so you have the advantage!

Your job is to deny them the chance to take your advantage away from you by continually strengthening and building the relationship.

Fact: It's a mistake to leave this to your staff because being fallible human beings, they **won't** do it consistently.

You have to communicate clearly regularly and consistently and we've already talked about lots of tools you can use to do it with, back in Secret number 1.

Just remember that whatever you communicate has to be valuable to your clients. It needs to be newsworthy and either educate them or make them an offer that shows you care.

You need to make sure when you communicate that you focus on what's in it for them because that's what they're interested in.

This means for example, if you've got a new product to talk about:

- *Tell them about the problem it solves.*

- *Tell them about the money they'll save.*

- *Tell them about how it's going to make them feel.*

- *Tell them about the results other people have been getting with it.*

- *Tell them about the guarantee you're offering with it.*

- *Make them an offer they can't refuse!*

That's what they want to hear from you.

Secret Number 3.

Understand Your **'Unique Perceived Benefit'.**

This is not a phrase most of us have heard of so you're probably wondering what I'm talking about, but it's simple really.

Your **'Unique Perceived Benefit' (UPB)** is a statement you use to make your salon stand out from the crowd, so it will be seen as **DIFFERENT** from your competitors. Don't you think it would be great if your salon stood out from the crowd?

Of course it would!!

Now occasionally, when you look at what you do, you'll find your UPB is obvious, but in most cases you need to 'create' it from scratch and I'll show you how in a moment.

Once you've done it though:

- *Your UPB becomes your catchphrase or motto.*

- *It becomes the thing you're 'known' for.*

- *Your job is to spread your UPB message clearly and consistently in a way your marketplace can't ignore.*

I can't stress enough how important this is to you.

How can you expect people to choose you, over and above any other salon, if they can't quickly see what it is you do that's so right for them?

If you'd like to see an example, then go to my salon's website at **www.stevehilliardhairdressing.**com and you'll see my UPB communicated very clearly above the fold on the home page and it's our **4 Point Client Guarantee.**

If you visit one of my salons you'll find the **4 Point Client Guarantee** communicated clearly on the outside and on the inside as well.

Our systems are set up to measure, whether the **4 Point Client Guarantee** is being delivered consistently.

Our salon pay structure is structured to reward the team members who most consistently deliver on the **4 Point Client Guarantee.**

I could go on, but hopefully by now you realise that I walk the talk on this and having a powerful UPB is an absolute must when it comes to **'Doing'** clear communication!

You'll have probably noticed my UPB included a guarantee.

A lot of salon owners are afraid to give a guarantee but it has many benefits and here are just a few.

Getting over the fear of giving a guarantee:

- *Raises your standards and gives you a reputation to live up to.*

- *Gives you valuable feedback about problems, because more clients will **bother** to tell you if they're not happy: At the moment most unhappy clients just go home and tell everyone else, which is **not** what you want!*

- *Encourages far more 'new' clients to come in and give you a try because your guarantee will give them confidence.*

So remember that fear isn't real and get past the thing that worries most salon owners when I suggest they use a guarantee, which is they're afraid clients will rip them off.

All the research shows very few actually do. If you've got the guts to offer one you'll get a better salon **and** lots of new clients.

I hope you understand that a strong UPB helps you communicate clearly that you're not the same as other salons.

This is **critical.**

Why?

Well, if you're not seen as different, what do you think becomes the most important factor people base their choice on?

That's right... **price!**

Your UPB takes you out of the 'price war' because you're no longer seen as the **same** as other salons!

Secret Number 4.

Find out what you're up against by mystery shopping your competitors' salons... and your own as well!

It pays to be aware of the standards your competitors are setting, and mystery shopping is a great way to find out.

- *You can do this before you open, as I did when I sized up my competition before opening in Ampthill.*

- *You can do it when new competitors open as well, to find out if you need to up your game!*

- *You can do it to understand why your own salon isn't performing as you want it to but you're not sure why.*

So, by now I hope you can see that mystery shopping is a very useful tool and the good news is it's simple to set up a program.

Get together a small group of people who love having their hair done and are capable of writing a report afterwards.

Brief them on what you're looking for and give them a questionnaire to fill in after their visit.

I have a mystery shopper form as part of my *"Do Something*

Different Success System" and I'll let you know how you can get hold of a free copy at the end of the book.

Once you've briefed your Mystery Shoppers, get them to make and keep an appointment and then give them 2 days **max** to fill in the form. Then you can sit down with them, go over their notes and see what you've learned.

It's all common sense, isn't it. And taking the time to do this will confirm what you're doing well and open your eyes to possible opportunities you might be missing.

By the way, I meant what I said about mystery shopping your own salon as well.

Another pair of eyes looking at what's going on won't do any harm! Research has shown that the quality of hairdressing you offer is surprisingly low on a client's list of priorities. They're likely to be more concerned about feeling comfortable, how clean and well organised your salon is and whether you keep them waiting.

Mystery shopping will give you a lot of valuable information about all these things.

Secret Number 5.

Communicate your marketing message clearly using the power of direct response communication.

Direct response communication is exactly what the name

suggests; its communication you **know** clients have **'responded'** to.

This means having a **'call to action'** that can easily be measured, at the end of your marketing communication.

So for example, if you were giving away £5 Gift Vouchers to new clients and to get one, clients had to call the salon using a special tracking number, which is cheap and easy to set up, you'd easily be able to measure the response and know if the offer worked or not.

Secret Number 6.

Tap into the power of 'FREE'.

We mentioned **'FREE'** earlier but let's just spell it out for you in more detail. When you give your clients the 'little extras' and 'nice touches' you add a great deal of 'emotion' to your relationship and it can make a big difference.

I've seen salons give clients:

- *A rose at valentines.*

- *An Easter Egg at Easter time.*

- *A Birthday card with a £10 voucher.*

- *A Christmas card with a thank you letter and some vouchers to keep us busy in January and February.*

What little gifts could you give your clients throughout the year?

You can also add power to communication with offers that are based on the word **'free'**.

It's not only new clients who respond to free.

You can modify or re-enforce your existing client's behaviour by giving give them free stuff, if they do what you want.

For example in my salon if you book your next 3 appointments as you leave we'll enter you into a monthly prize draw to win your next appointment for FREE.

The permutations are endless but never underestimate the power of free. Research has shown it's the most effective word you can use in your communication and relationship building efforts.

OK, we've covered a lot of different ideas about how to **'DO Clear Communication'** in this chapter, haven't we? But here's one last thought.

If you do communicate clearly and consistently it's easy to find you've become 20% more successful at:

1. *Attracting new clients;*

2. *Getting existing clients to spend more;*

3. *Getting existing clients to come in more frequently;*

4. *Keeping existing clients loyal to you for longer.*

If you do become 20% more successful all those things you'll find your turnover has more than doubled!

Let's do the sums and prove it.

Let's make it easy to calculate so imagine your salon has:

- *1000 clients who spend.*

- *£30 per visit and come in.*

- *5 times per year and stay loyal for.*

- *5 years.*

Your sum looks like this:

1000 clients X £30 spend X 5 visits x 5 years = £750,000

Now let's improve all those figures by **'only' 20%**

- *1000 clients + 20% becomes 1200.*

- *£30 +20% becomes £36.*

- *5 visits + 20% becomes 6 visits.*

- *5 years loyalty + 20% becomes 6 years; which means the total number of visits your average client makes goes up from 25 to 36.*

So your new sum looks like this:

1200 clients X £36 spend X 36 visits x 5 years = £1,555,200

An improvement of 101.6%.

And that's not all; the value of each new client you attracted has gone up as well! Look at the figures and you'll see.

Before we improved everything by just **20%** an **'average'** client came in **25** times and spent **£30** making them worth **£750.**

After we improved everything by just 20% ... an average client comes in 36 times and spends £36 making them worth £1296.

So by making a small improvement in several areas, every new client is suddenly worth 68% more:

WOW!

Now do you see why **'DOING CLEAR COMMUNICATION'** isn't an optional extra we can afford to leave to the gossip mongers!

Now do you see why it's a **MASSIVE** mistake to simply focus on attracting new clients when you should also spend just as much time growing your existing clients:

- *Frequency of visit.*

- *Average spend.*

- *Loyalty!*

I hope so!

CHAPTER 6

'DO' long lasting success!

Can you remember meeting someone special for the **first time and thinking WOW,** nice looks, great body, and warm smile; you *really were <u>attracted</u> to this person.*

But later, when you got to know them better, their annoying habits and different values started to emerge. You discovered they were not the person you thought they were *and you're left looking for a way out of the relationship!*

In the beginning they had **'The 'X factor',** that indefinable **'something'** that attracted you, *but it didn't last!*

You don't want people being turned off, you want everyone to be attracted, don't you.

When I say we want **'everyone'** to be attracted to your salon; I mean you, your staff and your clients. To understand how we make it happen for 'everyone' we need answers to these questions:

- *What would make a salon owner want to keep a business for a life time?*

- *What would make staff want to work there for their whole career?*

- *What would make clients want to stay loyal to a salon and rave about it to their friends?*

They're good questions, so let's dig a bit deeper. Would you feel your salon has the **'X factor'** if you were:

- *Making lots of money?*

- *Working for as much or little time as you want?*

- *Working with a team of people who you respect and trust because they're low maintenance and work hard?*

- *Only doing the things you find 'fun' and 'enjoyable' because everything else was being done for you?*

- *Recognised within the industry as being a success?*

Do you think your staff would feel your salon has the **'X factor'** if they were:

- *Well paid?*

- *Well trained?*

- *Trusted and appreciated?*

- *Treated fairly?*

- *Given responsibility?*

- *Encouraged to aspire to and attain career goals?*

Do you think your clients would feel your salon has the **'X factor'** if it was:

- *A place where they feel important?*

- *Managed by people who understand what they want and deliver it consistently?*

- *Comfortable, friendly and easy to belong to?*

- *Staffed by people they like and respect?*

- *A place where they get value for money?*

A salon that could deliver all that, to all those **different** people, would be a pretty special place wouldn't it? It would certainly be a salon that everyone would have an emotional bond with. It would have that indefinable something that would attract people and keep them loyal. I think by any standard of measurement it would have **'The X Factor'.**

By the way, I want you to notice I've put the 3 groups we've just talked about in a very specific order:

- *The owner first.*

- *Then the staff.*

- *Finally the clients.*

Let me ask *"Does this seem back to front to you?"*

Why am I asking? Because I often ask salon owners this question, and **99%** of the time they tell me I've got it wrong *they think the clients should come first on the list.*

Let me explain why I believe that's an expensive mistake and why it would pay you to look at it the other way round. A salon doesn't just **happen.** Someone has to have the idea, get the money together and take the risk. That someone is the owner.

No owner = no salon = no jobs = no clients.

See what I mean? It all starts with the owner; a salon **'has'** to meet the needs of the owner first. If it doesn't, *in the long run the business will either be sold or die a long lingering death!*

Do you need more proof that the owner's feelings are the most important? Well, try looking at it this way.

If an owner isn't X factor happy:

- *They won't be an X factor boss.*

- *They won't attract X factor staff.*

- *Clients won't get X factor service!*

So for staff and clients to be X factor happy in the long run, *the owner has to be X factor happy first.*

Put another way.

X factor clients can only be looked after by X factor staff and X factor staff will only work for an X factor boss.

It all comes back to you and making sure you get the X factor first. You'll then make sure your staff get it. They'll then make damn sure they give X factor service to their clients because it's the best way of keeping their X factor job with an X factor boss.

The X factor starts and ends with you!

There's a reason why we've tackled the X factor lesson last, and it's because most of the tools you need to use to give your salon **'The X Factor'** have already been given to you as we've learned about the previous 6 mistakes. We needed to understand them first before we could add this last piece to the jigsaw.

So let's remind ourselves of what we've already covered, then we can add the missing piece *although I've already given you a BIG hint as to what it is.*

An X factor boss:

- *Has a positive self-image.*

- *Sticks to their 'strengths' and delegates round their weaknesses.*

- *Only employs people with the right attitude, values and behaviour, doesn't try to please or placate the 'Number 3s' but politely and with respect moves them on.*

- *Knows how to avoid the trap of continually employing the wrong people, only to discover their mistake later.*

- *Has a salon that makes sense as a 'business', with effective systems in place to 'measure' the key performance indicators, so they know if it's performing well whether they are there or not.*

- *Has an effective 'marketing system' in place, so the business is continually spreading a positive news agenda that attracts new clients and rewards existing clients.*

That's a brief summary of what we've covered so far, isn't it… *so what's missing?*

What's been implied and suggested, but not spelt out? What's the glue that holds everything together? I'll tell you. *"The missing ingredient is found in the principles of EQ."*

Not sure what EQ is?

It's the measurement of 'Emotional Intelligence' which is our ability to understand and communicate with the emotions of other people. People who are intelligent have a high IQ; people who are emotionally intelligent have a high EQ.

If your business is designed to meet the emotional needs of you, your staff and your clients, **then it will really have the X factor!**

Why is it so important?

Because all the research shows that emotions drive human behaviour, *NOT LOGIC.*

Go back to the list of things that **'X factor'** bosses, staff and clients want and you'll see it's littered with emotion words such as:

- *Like.*

- *Trust.*

- *Respect.*

- *Appreciate.*

The good news is that while your IQ score stays much the same throughout your life, your EQ score can rise dramatically if you do the right things! What are the right things? Just about everything I've shared with you in this book, *that's what makes it so <u>powerful!</u>*

You'll find your EQ will grow when you:

- *Feel good about who you are and what you want.*

- *Focus on what you're good at.*

- *Surround yourself with people who you trust and can work with.*

- *Organise your business properly.*

- *Communicate clearly and positively with everyone.*

Fact: It will pay you more than you can ever imagine to develop a high EQ for yourself, because a high EQ business will follow, like night follows day.

Your high EQ business will have **'The X Factor'** and you'll get:

- *The staff.*

- *The clients.*

- *The salon.*

- *And the life you've always wanted and will **definitely deserve.***

If you want to understand more, much more, about developing your EQ I'd recommend a book called: **Primal Leadership;** *realising the power of emotional intelligence* by Daniel Goleman.

What's next for you?

Believe me when I say, if you make a commitment to begin consistently **'Doing Something Different In Your Salon every day'** it will have a **'huge'** effect on your performance; and will lead you to a highly profitable, fulfilling salon, more rapidly than you **ever** expected.

But there's a question you need to ask: **"Do you have the time and skills to do it on your own?"**

If your answer is **'yes'** then great. You've got the book as a guide. All you need to **'DO'** is act!

Nothing happens without action, does it, and I wish you every success.

On the other hand, if you feel you don't have the time to put everything together, or you can't see how you're going to get started, you might want to take a closer look at my *"Do Something Different Success System".*

When you do, you'll see it's been designed to take the pressure off **you.** Once that happens you'll find your salon starts working better very quickly.

If you take advantage of my *"Do Something Different Success*

System" you'll soon have a salon that's working properly because all your:

- *Marketing*

- *health and safety*

- *staff recruitment*

- *staff training*

- *staff motivation*

- *artistic leadership*

- *customer service and strategic planning responsibilities* will be properly organised.

This will have a **'huge'** effect on your performance and how you feel about your salon.

The really good news is you can try my *"Do Something Different Success System"* program and the support you get with it, safe in the knowledge that you're covered by my **Cast Iron, 12 month, 100% Money Back Guarantee.**

This means it's <u>**impossible**</u> to lose by trying it and if you've been paying attention, you'll have noticed… **I've just given you the great example of a UPB in action I promised you earlier!**

I've just made you an offer and given you a guarantee… haven't I!

If you feel my offer and the guarantee look like something you want to know more about, send an Email with the subject line **"I want to do something different in my salon Steve"** to… **info@stevehilliardcoaching.com** and I'll contact you for an informal, no obligation chat. Please remember that places on the *"Do Something Different Success System"* program are limited, so it will pay you to act quickly if you want a slot!

Here's a final thought I want to leave you with.

You now know all the power of doing something different, your future is in front of you; you have a choice… and its **decision** time.

Are you going to be one of the salon owners who read a book like this and then decides to **'DO'… absolutely nothing!**

Or are you going to step up to the mark and decide to:

- *Take control of your self-image.*

- *Take control of your salon.*

- *Take control of your life by getting and **'Doing Something Different'** and stepping confidently into your **'X factor'** future!*

I hope so because, as I'm sure you'll remember:

> *"If you keep on doing what you've always done, You'll keep on getting what you've always got!"*

Is that what you **_really_** want?

Postscript

I've shared some of my powerful *"Do Something Different Success System"* tools with you in this book and promised you **FREE** copies of my **'Quarterly Budget Sheet'** and **'Mystery Shopper Survey'.**

If you'd like either of those visit www.freesalonforms.com and you can download them from there.